Pit Boss Wood Pellet Grill Cookbook

Delicious & Cheap Porks' Recipes Ready in Less Than 30 Minutes for Beginners and Advanced Pitmasters

John Patch

4

TABLE OF CONTENTS

Sommario

Introduction

In the culinary field, we are always looking for valid solutions to have multifunctional kitchen tools. These multifunctional tools must be able to cook in different ways and with all possible ingredients.

Without neglecting one of the favorite cooking methods, especially with regard to meat: grilling.

In addition, what better solution could that be than the Pit Boss?

The Pit Bosses are in fact grills and smokers that allow different types of cooking. They are charcoal grills and outdoor smokers that use pellets as a combustion Medium. It is well known that pellets as a combustion material, compared to gas or electrical systems, are an environmentally friendly solution. This makes this product a much greener choice for cooking. What exactly is the pellet? Pellet is a biofuel made up of pressed wooden cylinders obtained from wood processing waste.

As with any purchase, purchasing a pellet grill requires a number of criteria that must be followed if you are to make the right decision. Although everyone's cooking needs are different, it is necessary to consider various criteria before concluding the search, such as size, price, and ease of installation, temperature control and efficiency.

So based on these criteria, to what extent is the Pit Boss among the best choices?

As regards the specific point of size, the Pit Boss falls within the Medium-high range of pellet grills. If you have a large family or often invite friends and family for lunch or dinner, Pit Bosses are big enough to meet your needs. On the other hand, if you have large quantities of food to grill, the Pit Boss is certainly one of the ideal choices.

As for the price, if you are looking for an affordable pellet grill, the Pit Boss is the ideal alternative. In fact, the Pit Bosses fall within the average price ranges. It is certainly not cheap, but compared to the competitors it is much cheaper. In addition, if you are a beginner and have a fairly limited budget, Pit Bosses are an option to really consider.

As for temperature control, Pit Bosses have a temperature range from 180 ° F to 500 ° F. and it is quite accurate within 5 degrees of the temperature you have preset. Then you can smoke the meat at less than 200 ° F or you can use the higher temperatures to cook pizzas or bread. An arched drip plate helps in creating warmer "cooking zones" for grilled meats, and a function of forced convection ensures that the meat is sealed properly.

Another side to consider is a number of additional features that give Pit Bosses a competitive edge. Auto-start function and digital control with LED reading panel are standard, but the included meat probe allows for a greater control over ingredients.

In addition, various types of food can be cooked, even the most delicate ones such as fish.

Also not to be overlooked is the fact that the use of flavored pellets give a particular and more intense flavor to your dishes.

What are Pit Boss main benefits?

The advantages of using these barbecues are many:

- First of all, environmental: the pellets as we said are the waste product of wood processing, so there is no need to cut down the trees.
- High yield in cooking: wood in pellets is characterized by a high calorific value, capable of producing heat quickly and, above all, of maintaining it for a long time.
- Quick and easy: the control panel allows you to set the type of cooking and the temperature. To turn on the pellet barbecue just press the button and wait a few minutes to reach the preset temperature.
- Temperature Control and Maintenance: the thermo regulator controls the temperature and, above all, keeps it constant throughout the cooking cycle.
- Uniform cooking: thanks to the ventilation system, the food is cooked by convention, at a constant temperature. The result is uniform, balanced cooking.
- Quality cooking: cooking with pellets allows you to keep the taste and flavor of food unaltered. Natural cooking, a new generation wood cooking.
- Minimal ash residues: the pellets, after combustion, leave minimal ash residues. An aspect that facilitates the ritual cleaning of the barbecue.
- Better flavors: as we have seen The Pit Boss barbeque uses one hundred percent natural wood pellets and is able to give the food the same flavor that cooking with wood would bring. Furthermore, as we said previously, being flavored pellets makes a greater contribution to flavor your dishes.

- It is a reliable product: The materials with which the elements that make up its structure have been made also guarantee the total reliability of the product itself, making it safe and long lasting. This company, in fact, sells very good products in this field, made from the best materials.

What kind of pellets?

We know that Pit Boss working is based on pellet burning. These clean-burning barbecue wood pellets generate about 8200 BTUs per pound with very little ash, a low moisture content (5-7%), and are carbon neutral.

Barbecue wood pellets are produced by pure raw material (sawdust) being pulverized with a hammer mill and the material is pushed through a die with pressure. As the pellet is forced through the die, it is cut, cooled, screened, vacuumed, and then bagged for consumer use. However, which are the best pellets to use?

- **HICKORY BLEND**
  Rich, smoky bacon-like flavor. Considered the "Kings of the Woods"
- **CHERRY BLEND**
  Slightly sweet, but also tart. It gives a rosy tint to light meals
- **MESQUITE BLEND**
  Strong, tangy, spicy flavor. Think Tex-Mex cuisine.
- **WHISKEY BARREL BLEND**
  Strong, sweet smoke with aromatic tang. Perfect for red meats.
- **APPLE BLEND**
  Smoky, mild sweetness flavor. Highly recommended for baking
- **COMPETITION BLEND**
  A perfect blend of sweet, savory, and tart. Used by many professional grillers

How to cook with the Pit Boss

After explaining what the Pit Boss is, how it works, the advantages and the pellets to use, we will now show you which methods to use for cooking with it.

Wanting to simplify as much as possible, in order to make it clear right away even to newbies what we are talking about, we can say that there are basically 3 main cooking techniques that can be achieved with the Pit Boss.

Specifically, they are:

- Direct cooking,
- Indirect cooking,
- Smoking (hot) is also known as barbecue or American "low & slow" cooking.

Direct cooking

Direct cooking is the cooking method that we all know and consists of the classic "grilled". To carry out this type of cooking, the food must be placed on the grill in correspondence with the embers.

Cooking takes place by direct and "violent" heat radiation and by conduction of the grill, usually in steel or cast iron. With direct cooking, very high temperatures are reached, sometimes even higher than 500° F, which allows us to quickly cook small pieces of meat such as sausages, skewers, ribs, steaks.

The distinctive feature of this cooking is the grill marks, that is those splendid and scenographic dark lines that the grill leaves where it is in direct contact with the food (heat by conduction).

This phenomenon has a very specific name and is due to the Maillard reaction.

The main difficulty of direct cooking is the flames, so it is necessary to know how to master them in order not to ruin everything. The flare-ups are mainly due to the fat that melts and drips onto the hot embers or the burner's flame. The solution is the correct use of the lid; it will be enough to close the barbecue with the lid, thus limiting the access of oxygen, to extinguish the flames immediately.

Indirect cooking

Indirect cooking is the system that comes closest to how an oven works.

To be able to cook indirectly, it is necessary to "literally" divide our barbecue into 2 distinct areas:

- on one side the embers or the burner lit in the case of a gas barbecue.
- On the other, a completely free area, without embers or with the burner off.

The food is placed on the grill on the opposite side to the coals or with the burner on. By closing the lid, we will have a closed system where the heat does not directly affect the food, but thanks to the air motions, it circulates inside the chamber—cooking by sweetly cooking our dish and indirectly by convection of heat.

Indirect cooking takes longer than direct cooking but allows you to cook large pieces of meat such as a roast, a whole chicken or a salmon without running the risk of burning the outside while cooking the inside perfectly while maintaining the natural juiciness of the food.

Smoked cooking

Smoking, barbecue or low & slow cooking: convection of heat with the presence of smoke

Low temperature for very long times, these are the rules of a low & slow barbecue cooking.

It is nothing more than indirect cooking carried out at very low temperatures; the range goes from 194° F to 248° F, where the presence of smoking always characterizes the distinctive feature.

With this cooking method, you can cook any cut of meat, even large ones, always obtaining very tender and juicy foods. Obviously, even this technique is always carried out with the lid closed; the food cooks by convection with the added value of the unmistakable aroma of the Pit Boss guaranteed by the presence of smoke induced by the partial combustion of aromatic pellets.

In conclusion, each technique is used to achieve a precise result, but often the best is achieved by combining several different cooking methods within the same preparation:

- Direct cooking to create a nice burnished and fragrant crust perhaps with nice grill marks.
- Indirect cooking to achieve the ideal degree of cooking of the food.

Shopping list

Here is a good shopping list to be able to cook with your Pit Boss.

All you will need for our recipes will be:

- First of all meat: choose it from the best quality and your trusted butcher. Among the best meats to cook in the Pit Boss, choose veal, beef, pork, chicken, turkey and duck.
- High quality fish: you should choose very fresh and good quality fish. From shrimps to salmon tuna or cod you can cook every kind of fish.
- Cheeses: every kind of cheese could be cooked in the Pit Boss
- Quality vegetables and fruit: if they are of organic origin even better, but the grilled vegetables with the Pit Boss will be delicious. Choose from all kinds: from green ones to eggplants, bell peppers and so on. For what about fruits you can choose any type.
- Spices and aromatic herbs: they can never be missing to flavor your dishes. From thyme, oregano and rosemary to sweeter or spicier spices.
- Fats: you will need olive oil, vegetable oils, butter and margarine to make delicious dishes

Recipes

Pork

Pork tenderloin with spring onion sauce

PREPARATION TIME: 20 minutes
COOKING TIME: 20 minutes
DIFFICULT LEVEL: Simple
CALORIES FOR 100 GRAMS: 393
FAT FOR 100 GRAMS: 19
CARBOIDRATES FOR 100 GRAMS: 9
PROTEINS FOR 100 GRAMS: 23

INGREDIENTS FOR 4 SERVINGS
- 1 pork fillet of 800 grams
- 60 ml of White Wine
- 8 slices of smoked bacon
- 16 sage leaves
- Salt and pepper to taste
- Olive oil to taste

For the spring onion sauce
- 8 spring onions
- 50 grams of butter
- 30 ml of white wine
- Salt and pepper to taste

DIRECTIONS
1. Preheat the Pit Boss to 250 ° F.
2. Washing and drying the pork tenderloin.
3. Wash and dry sage and rosemary.
4. In a bowl put salt, pepper, olive oil and white wine.
5. Brush the fillet with the emulsion.
6. Roll up the pork fillet with the slices of bacon.
7. Now cover the meat with the sage leaves and stop them by tying them with a kitchen string.
8. Put the fillet directly on the grill and cook for 20 minutes.
9. In the meantime, prepare the onion sauce.
10. Remove the final part of the spring onions, then wash them and

cut them into 4 parts.

11. Melt the butter in a pan and then put the spring onions to brown.

12. At this point, blend with the white wine. Once the wine has evaporated, turn off the heat and keep them warm.

13. After 20 minutes, check the internal temperature of the meat.

14. If it has reached 145 ° F then remove it from the grill, otherwise continue for another 2 minutes.

15. Just cooked, put it on a cut and let the meat rest for 5 minutes.

16. Now remove the kitchen string, and cut the fillet into slices and place it on serving plates.

17. Add the spring onions, sprinkle the meat with the cooking juices and serve.

Grilled pork skewers

PREPARATION TIME: 15 minutes + 1hour to rest in fridge
COOKING TIME: 8 minutes
DIFFICULT LEVEL: Simple
CALORIES FOR 100 GRAMS: 134
FAT FOR 100 GRAMS: 7
CARBOIDRATES FOR 100 GRAMS: 12
PROTEINS FOR 100 GRAMS: 23

INGREDIENTS FOR 4 SERVINGS

- 400 grams of pork loin
- 400 grams of pineapple pulp
- 2 tablespoons of mustard
- 2 tablespoons of balsamic vinegar
- 2 teaspoons of honey
- 1 teaspoon of chopped chives
- Olive oil to taste
- Salt and pepper to taste

DIRECTIONS

1. Wash and dry the pineapple and then cut it into cubes.
2. Wash and dry the loin and then cut it into cubes, the same size as the pineapple.
3. Prepare the skewers by alternately sticking dice of meat and pineapple into the wooden sticks.
4. In a large bowl, mix the mustard, vinegar, honey, oil, chives, salt and pepper.
5. Put the skewers in the bowl; seal it with cling film and leave to marinate for an hour in the refrigerator.
6. Preheat the grill of your Pit Boss to 200°F.
7. After marinating time, drain the skewers and place them on the grill.
8. Grill the skewers for 8 minutes, turning them on all sides.
9. Just ready, remove them from the grill, put them on plates and serve immediately.

Pork loin with grappa

PREPARATION TIME: 25 minutes+ 3 hours of marinating
COOKING TIME: 90 minutes
DIFFICULT LEVEL: Simple
CALORIES FOR 100 GRAMS: 231
FAT FOR 100 GRAMS: 9
CARBOIDRATES FOR 100 GRAMS: 3
PROTEINS FOR 100 GRAMS: 27

INGREDIENTS FOR 4 SERVINGS

- 1 kilo of pork loin
- 1 clove of garlic
- half a shallot
- 1 sprig of thyme
- 1 sprig of rosemary
- 100 ml of grappa
- 4 juniper berries
- 100 ml of white wine
- 200 ml of meat broth
- Olive oil to taste
- Salt and pepper to taste

DIRECTIONS

1. Wash and dry the pork loin and remove excess fat.
2. Brush the meat with olive oil.
3. Wash and dry the thyme and rosemary and then chop them.
4. Put the pork loin in the bowl and then sprinkle the entire surface with salt, pepper and aromatic herbs.
5. Peel the garlic and shallots and then chop them. Put them in the bowl with the pork.
6. Finally add the juniper berries and sprinkle everything with wine and grappa.
7. Cover the bowl with transparent paper and marinate the pork for 3 hours.
8. Preheat the Pit Boss at 338 ° F for 15 minutes with the lid closed.

9. Drain the marinade from the roast, place it on the grill and proceed with indirect cooking for about an hour and a half.
10. Close the lid. It is not necessary to turn the roast.
11. Remove the meat from the barbecue and let it rest for at least 10-15 minutes covered with a sheet of aluminium foil to absorb the juices.
12. Meanwhile, strain the marinade in a saucepan and reduce it by half.
13. Now cut the pork into slices.
14. Put the slices on serving plates, sprinkle with the marinating liquid and serve.

Pulled pork with potatoes and onions

PREPARATION TIME: 25 minutes+ 3 hours of marinating
COOKING TIME: 90 minutes
DIFFICULT LEVEL: Simple
CALORIES FOR 100 GRAMS: 380
FAT FOR 100 GRAMS: 21
CARBOIDRATES FOR 100 GRAMS: 11
PROTEINS FOR 100 GRAMS: 23

INGREDIENTS FOR 4 SERVINGS

- 1.5 kg of pork shoulder
- 1 minced clove of garlic
- 1 chopped chilli
- 1 tablespoon of cumin
- 2 tablespoons of paprika
- 1 tablespoon of mustard powder
- 4 potatoes
- 4 onions
- Olive oil to taste
- Salt and pepper to taste

DIRECTIONS

1. In a bowl mix garlic, chilli, sugar, salt, pepper, mustard, cumin and paprika.
2. Wash and dry the pork shoulder. Brush it with oil and then sprinkle the entire surface with the spice mix.
3. Put a handful of hickory and cherry chips in the smoked box.
4. Now preheat the Pit Boss at 257 ° F for 10 minutes.
5. When the temperature reaches 125 degrees and there is smoke, open the lid and place the meat in the centre of the grill.
6. Close the lid and cook for 7 hours.
7. After 7 hours check the cooking and if it has, reached 188 ° F, remove it from the Pit Boss and let it rest for 15-30 minutes, wrapped in foil.

8. Meanwhile, cook the potatoes and onions.
9. Peel the potatoes, wash them thoroughly under running water and then cut them into cubes.
10. Peel the onions and cut them into slices.
11. Put them in a roasting pan brushed with olive oil.
12. Raise the Pit Boss temperature to 320 ° F and close the lid.
13. Place the potatoes and onions on the grill and cook for 15 minutes, with the lid closed.
14. As soon as they are cooked, remove the vegetables from the barbecue.
15. Now cut the meat and put it on the plates. Garnish with the potatoes and onions and serve.

Pork skewers with ginger

PREPARATION TIME: 20 minutes+1 night of marinating
COOKING TIME: 15 minutes
DIFFICULT LEVEL: Simple
CALORIES FOR 100 GRAMS: 320
FAT FOR 100 GRAMS: 7
CARBOIDRATES FOR 100 GRAMS: 8
PROTEINS FOR 100 GRAMS: 24

INGREDIENTS FOR 4 SERVINGS

- 500 grams of pork loin
- 16 cherry tomatoes
- 1 tablespoon of balsamic vinegar
- 40 ml of soy sauce
- 40 grams of grated ginger
- 40 grams of honey
- 1 orange
- Olive oil to taste
- Salt and pepper to taste

DIRECTIONS

1. Wash and dry the pork and then cut it into cubes.
2. Wash and dry the cherry tomatoes.
3. Wash and dry the orange and then grate the zest and strain the juice into a bowl.
4. Put in the bowl with the orange, honey, soy sauce, balsamic vinegar and olive oil and mix everything well.
5. Add the pork cubes and mix to flavour well.
6. Refrigerate and leave to marinate overnight.
7. After the marinating time, take the meat and drain it.
8. Wash and dry the cherry tomatoes.
9. Now start forming the skewers. Take 4 metal skewers and put first a cube of meat and then a tomato. Repeat the same operation until the end of all the ingredients.

10. Preheat the Pit Boss at 392 ° F for 10 minutes.
11. Now put the skewers directly on the grill and cook them over indirect heat for about 15 minutes.
12. Turn the skewers often and as soon as they are cooked, remove them from the grill and let them rest for 5 minutes.
13. Now put the skewers on the plates and serve.

Grilled pork tenderloin with oranges and limes

PREPARATION TIME: 20 minutes
COOKING TIME: 40 minutes
DIFFICULT LEVEL: Medium
CALORIES FOR 100 GRAMS: 176
FAT FOR 100 GRAMS: 10
CARBOIDRATES FOR 100 GRAMS: 3
PROTEINS FOR 100 GRAMS: 22

INGREDIENTS FOR 4 SERVINGS
- 1 kilo of pork tenderloin
- 4 sprigs of rosemary
- the juice of an orange
- 1 shallot
- 1 carrot
- 4 sprigs of thyme
- 1 clove of garlic
- 150 ml of meat broth
- Salt and pepper to taste
- Olive oil to taste

DIRECTIONS
1. Peel and wash the shallot, garlic and carrot and then chop them.
2. Pass to the meat now: First, place the pork tenderloin on a cutting board and remove excess fat and tendons.
3. Now wash and dry the fillet. Tie the pork with kitchen string.
4. Wash and dry the rosemary and then place it between the string and the meat.
5. Now brush the meat with olive oil and then sprinkle all the meat with salt and pepper.
6. Preheat the Pit Boss to 352 ° F with the lid closed for 15 minutes.
7. Heat a cast iron saucepan for 10 minutes on indirect heat.
8. After 10 minutes, put two tablespoons of olive oil in the saucepan and let it heat up.

9. Add the garlic and brown it for a couple of minutes.
10. Now add the fillet and brown it for 4 minutes, turning it on all sides.
11. Now add the orange juice and continue cooking for 5 minutes.
12. Now add the shallot and carrot.
13. Stir, season with salt and pepper and continue for another 5 minutes.
14. Now add the broth and cook for 25 minutes.
15. Check the cooking inside the meat and if it has reached 158 ° F. remove the fillet from the barbecue otherwise continue until the temperature is reached.
16. Once cooked, remove from the barbecue and let it rest for 5 minutes.
17. Remove the string and cut the fillet into slices.
18. Blend the cooking juices with an immersion blender.
19. Put the slices of fillet on plates, sprinkle with the cooking juices and serve.

Pork fillet with honey and ginger

PREPARATION TIME: 15 minutes+2 hours of marinating
COOKING TIME: 15 minutes
DIFFICULT LEVEL: Simple
CALORIES FOR 100 GRAMS: 216
FAT FOR 100 GRAMS: 11
CARBOIDRATES FOR 100 GRAMS: 5
PROTEINS FOR 100 GRAMS: 23

INGREDIENTS FOR 4 SERVINGS

- 1 pork fillet of 600 grams
- 30 ml of soy sauce
- 30 ml of sesame oil
- 30 grams of grated ginger
- 40 grams of honey
- Salt and pepper to taste
- Olive oil to taste

DIRECTIONS

1. Start by eliminating the excess fat from the fillet and cut into pieces about 2 cm thick by cutting them lengthwise.
2. Wash and dry the fillets.
3. In a bowl put the soy sauce, ginger and honey. Stir until the honey has melted slightly.
4. Now add the sesame oil, olive oil, salt, pepper, and mix.
5. Now put the pork fillets inside the bowl and leave to marinate for 2 hours.
6. Preheat the Pit Boss at 338 ° F for 15 minutes with the lid closed.
7. Put the fillets and cook them for 15 minutes over Medium direct heat, with the lid closed.
8. Turn them every 5 minutes, and brush them with the marinating liquid.
9. As soon as they are cooked, remove them from the barbecue and let them rest for 5 minutes.

10. Put the marinade in a saucepan and let it reduce by half.
11. Put the fillets on plates, sprinkle them with the marinating liquid and serve.

BBQ pork belly

PREPARATION TIME: 15 minutes+4 hours of marinating
COOKING TIME: 2 hours
DIFFICULT LEVEL: Simple.
CALORIES FOR 100 GRAMS: 172
FAT FOR 100 GRAMS: 7
CARBOIDRATES FOR 100 GRAMS: 9
PROTEINS FOR 100 GRAMS: 17

INGREDIENTS FOR 4 SERVINGS

- 4 slices of pork belly 4 cm high
- 240 grams of barbecue sauce
- Salt and pepper to taste
- 1 sprig of chopped parsley

DIRECTIONS

1. Wash and dry the pork belly. Brush it with olive oil and then sprinkle all sides with salt and pepper.
2. Put the belly in a food bag; add the barbecue sauce and leave to marinate in the fridge for 4 hours.
3. After 4 hours, preheat the Pit Boss at 230 ° F for 15 minutes.
4. Put a handful of apple chips and a hickory in the smoked box.
5. Now put the pork belly directly on the grill, close the lid and let it smoke for 2 hours.
6. Add some chips after an hour.
7. When the meat reaches a core temperature of 161 ° F, you can remove the meat from the grill.
8. Let it rest for 5 minutes, then put on plates and serve.

Smoked pork fillet

PREPARATION TIME: 20 minutes
COOKING TIME: 2 hours
DIFFICULT LEVEL: Simple
CALORIES FOR 100 GRAMS: 177
FAT FOR 100 GRAMS: 4
CARBOIDRATES FOR 100 GRAMS: 9
PROTEINS FOR 100 GRAMS: 22

INGREDIENTS FOR 4 SERVINGS
- 1 whole pork fillet of 800 grams
- 1 tablespoon of paprika
- 1 tablespoon of dried thyme
- 1 tablespoon of dried rosemary
- 1 tablespoon of dried bay leaf
- 100 grams of barbecue sauce
- Salt and pepper to taste
- Olive oil to taste

DIRECTIONS
1. Preheat the Pit Boss at 230 ° F for 15 minutes with the lid closed.
2. Put in the smoked box and add a handful of cherry chips and whiskey blend.
3. In the meantime, remove any excess fat or silver film from the surface of the pork tenderloin.
4. Wash and dry the fillet, then brush the entire surface of the meat with olive oil.
5. Put the herbs, salt and spices in a bowl and mix well.
6. Sprinkle the entire surface of the meat with the rub.
7. Now put the fillet in the barbecue and let it smoke for 1 hour and 30 minutes.
8. At this point, brush the meat with the barbecue sauce and continue cooking for another 30 minutes.
9. After the two hours check the internal temperature of the meat

and if it is 145 ° F then remove from the barbecue, otherwise continue until the temperature is reached.

10. Just cooked, remove the fillet from the Pit Boss and let it rest for 5 minutes.

11. Now cut the fillet into slices put it on serving plates and serve with more barbecue sauce.

Pork ribs on the barbecue

PREPARATION TIME: 20 minutes+1 hour
COOKING TIME: 4 hours
DIFFICULT LEVEL: Medium
CALORIES FOR 100 GRAMS: 282
FAT FOR 100 GRAMS: 20
CARBOIDRATES FOR 100 GRAMS: 10
PROTEINS FOR 100 GRAMS: 26

INGREDIENTS FOR 4 SERVINGS
- 1 kilo of pork ribs
- 1 tablespoon of garlic powder
- 1 tablespoon of cumin
- 1 tablespoon of paprika
- 200 ml of apple cider vinegar
- 2 tablespoons of brown sugar
- 2 tablespoons of sriracha
- 2 tablespoons of ketchup
- Olive oil to taste
- Salt and pepper to taste

DIRECTIONS
1. Wash and dry the ribs and then place them in a large baking dish.
2. Put the pepper, salt, garlic powder, cumin and paprika in a bowl and then mix the spices well.
3. Spread the spice mixture on the ribs. Cover the pan with plastic wrap and put them to marinate for at least an hour.
4. Preheat the Pit Boss at 230 ° F for 15 minutes.
5. Put some cherry and hickory chips in the smoked box.
6. Now put the ribs on the grill and cook for 4 hours.
7. Add the chips every hour.
8. As soon as they are cooked, remove the ribs and let them rest for 15 minutes.

9. In the meantime, put a saucepan on the stove with the white wine vinegar, brown sugar, ketchup and sriracha.
10. Let it reduce on the heat until you get a sauce with a consistency similar to syrup.
11. Glaze the meat that you have taken from the grill with the sauce just made.
12. Cut the ribs into slices, put them on serving plates and serve.

Pork rolls with speck

PREPARATION TIME: 15 minutes
COOKING TIME: 20 minutes
DIFFICULT LEVEL: Simple
CALORIES FOR 100 GRAMS: 175
FAT FOR 100 GRAMS: 7
CARBOIDRATES FOR 100 GRAMS: 2
PROTEINS FOR 100 GRAMS: 24

INGREDIENTS FOR 4 SERVINGS
- 8 slices of pork loin of 150 grams each
- 8 slices of speck
- 8 sage leaves
- 330 ml of light beer
- Flour to taste
- Olive oil to taste
- Salt and pepper to taste

DIRECTIONS
1. Wash and dry the pork slices. Sprinkle the entire surface of the meat with salt and pepper.
2. Now put a slice of speck on each slice of pork.
3. Wash and dry the sage leaves. Close the rolls with toothpicks and adding a sage leaf between the toothpick and the meat.
4. Brush the rolls with olive oil and then pass them over the flour.
5. Preheat the Pit Boss at 338 ° F for 10 minutes with the lid closed.
6. Put a cast iron pan on direct heat and let it heat up.
7. Put two tablespoons of oil in the pan and as soon as it is hot, brown the rolls for a couple of minutes, turning them on all sides.
8. Add the beer to the pan, close the lid of the Pit Boss and continue cooking for another 15 minutes.
9. Just cooked, remove the rolls from the barbecue and let them rest for a couple of minutes.

10. Put the rolls on serving plates, sprinkle with the cooking juices and serve.

Pork ribs with paprika sauce

PREPARATION TIME: 20 minutes
COOKING TIME: 1 hour and 20 minutes
DIFFICULT LEVEL: Medium
CALORIES FOR 100 GRAMS: 364
FAT FOR 100 GRAMS: 31
CARBOIDRATES FOR 100 GRAMS: 5
PROTEINS FOR 100 GRAMS: 20

INGREDIENTS FOR 4 SERVINGS
- 800 grams of pork ribs
- 1 onion
- 1 carrot
- 2 tomatoes
- 1 potato
- 1 tablespoon of dried tarragon
- 20 grams of flour
- 250 ml of cooking cream
- 1 tablespoon of paprika
- Salt and pepper to taste
- Olive oil to taste

DIRECTIONS
1. Peel and wash the carrot and onion and then cut them into cubes.
2. Wash the tomatoes and cut them into cubes.
3. Brush a baking dish with olive oil and put the vegetables inside.
4. Sprinkle with tarragon.
5. Preheat the Pit Boss at 356 ° F for 10 minutes.
6. Put the vegetables in the barbecue and cook for 15 minutes.
7. Meanwhile, wash and dry the ribs and then brush them with olive oil.
8. Sprinkle with salt, pepper and paprika.
9. As soon as the vegetables are cooked, remove them from the

Pit Boss and place the ribs directly on the grill.

10. Cook for 50 minutes, with the lid closed.
11. At this point, turn them and continue cooking for another 50 minutes.
12. Check the cooking of the ribs and if it is 199 ° F then remove them from the Pit Boss, otherwise continue until the temperature is reached.
13. As soon as they are cooked, remove them from the Pit Boss and let them rest for 10 minutes.
14. In the meantime, put the vegetables in the glass of the mixer and blend them.
15. Put them in a saucepan and add the cream.
16. Stir, let it thicken for 10 minutes and then turn off.
17. Now cut the ribs, put them on plates, sprinkle them with the sauce and serve.

Pork chops with pumpkin cream

PREPARATION TIME: 25 minutes+ 2 hours of marinating
COOKING TIME: 40 minutes
DIFFICULT LEVEL: Simple
CALORIES FOR 100 GRAMS: 342
FAT FOR 100 GRAMS: 23
CARBOIDRATES FOR 100 GRAMS: 5
PROTEINS FOR 100 GRAMS: 21

INGREDIENTS FOR 4 SERVINGS
- 4 pork chops of 150 grams each
- 4 sage leaves
- 20 ml of soy sauce
- 1 tablespoon of brown sugar
- 1 sprig of rosemary
- 2 sprigs of thyme
- Salt and pepper to taste
- Olive oil to taste

For the sauce
- 500 grams of pumpkin
- 500 ml of vegetable broth
- 1 tsp ground cinnamon
- 1 teaspoon of nutmeg
- 1 potato
- Half a shallot
- Olive oil to taste
- Salt and pepper to taste

DIRECTIONS
1. Start with the chops. Wash and dry them and then put them in a baking dish.
2. Mix together the sugar, soy sauce, salt and pepper.
3. Put the emulsion over the chops and then add 4 tablespoons of olive oil.

4. Cover the dish with transparent paper and refrigerate for 2 hours.
5. Meanwhile, prepare the pumpkin cream.
6. Wash and dry the pumpkin pulp and then cut it into cubes.
7. Peel the potato, wash it thoroughly and then cut it into cubes.
8. Peel and wash the shallot and then chop it.
9. Heat a tablespoon of oil in a saucepan.
10. As soon as it is hot, put the onion to fry for a couple of minutes.
11. Once the onion is golden brown, add the pumpkin in the pan along with the potatoes.
12. Gradually add a few ladles of vegetable broth to cover the vegetables.
13. Season with salt, pepper, and cook for 30 minutes.
14. Once the vegetables are cooked, turn off the heat and begin to blend everything with an immersion mixer until you get a smooth and homogeneous cream. Add a sprinkling of nutmeg and cinnamon and mix everything. At this point, your pumpkin cream is ready, so set it aside.
15. Preheat the Pit Boss at 373 ° F for 10 minutes with the lid closed.
16. Cook the chops over direct heat with the lid closed, for 8-10 minutes, turning often until the meat reaches 149 ° F at the heart.
17. As soon as they are cooked, remove them from the barbecue and let them rest for 5 minutes.
18. Now turn the pan with the cream back on, let it heat for 5 minutes and then put the chops.
19. Cook well for 2 minutes and then turn off.
20. Put the chops on plates, sprinkle them with the pumpkin cream and serve.

Pork knuckle with barbecue sauce

PREPARATION TIME: 10 minutes+ 1 night of marinating
COOKING TIME: 5-7 hours
DIFFICULT LEVEL: Simple
CALORIES FOR 100 GRAMS: 272
FAT FOR 100 GRAMS: 10
CARBOIDRATES FOR 100 GRAMS: 5
PROTEINS FOR 100 GRAMS: 34

INGREDIENTS FOR 4 SERVINGS
- 800 grams of pork knuckle
- 1 bottle of white wine
- 1 sprig of rosemary
- 2 sprigs of thyme
- 1 red onion
- 100 grams of barbecue sauce
- Salt and pepper to taste
- Olive oil to taste

DIRECTIONS
1. Wash and dry the knuckle and then put it in a bowl.
2. Pour all the wine into the bowl, cover with transparent paper and marinate overnight.
3. After the marinating time, take the knuckle and dry it well.
4. Brush the shin first with oil and then with the barbecue sauce.
5. Wash and dry the rosemary and thyme and then chop them.
6. Sprinkle the entire surface of the meat with salt, pepper, thyme and rosemary.
7. Preheat the Pit Boss at 266 ° F for 15 minutes with the lid closed.
8. Put some apple chips and some hickory in the smoked box.
9. Put the knuckle on the grill in the middle, and let it smoke for 2 hours.
10. Insert more chips if necessary.
11. After two hours, remove the knuckle from the grill and wrap it on

2 sheets of aluminium foil.

12. Insert the thermometer into the meat of the shin being careful not to touch the bone.

13. Let the knuckle cook until it reaches a temperature of 205 ° F.

14. As soon as it is cooked, remove it from the grill and let it rest for an hour, always wrapped in aluminium foil.

15. Now you can open the aluminium foil and cut the knuckle into slices.

16. Put it on plates sprinkle with more barbecue sauce and serve.

Pork roast with apples

PREPARATION TIME: 45 minutes
COOKING TIME: 1 hour
DIFFICULT LEVEL: Medium
CALORIES FOR 100 GRAMS: 251
FAT FOR 100 GRAMS: 12
CARBOIDRATES FOR 100 GRAMS: 13
PROTEINS FOR 100 GRAMS: 18

INGREDIENTS FOR 4 SERVINGS
- 800 grams of pork loin
- 3 shallots
- 40 grams of Parmesan
- 100 ml of white wine
- 2 red apples
- 40 grams of breadcrumbs
- 40 grams of mustard
- Salt and pepper to taste
- Olive oil to taste

DIRECTIONS
1. Start by removing fat and silver skin from the pork loin.
2. Now wash it and dry it. Cut the pork loin in half by making an incision on one side of the meat at half height.
3. Sprinkle the meat with salt and pepper and set aside.
4. Peel and wash the shallots and then chop them.
5. Wash the apples, remove the core and seeds and then cut them into cubes.
6. Heat a tablespoon of oil in a pan and as soon as it is hot add the apples. Season with salt and pepper, stir and cook for 5 minutes.
7. Put the apples in a bowl and let them cool.
8. Now add the Parmesan and breadcrumbs and the chopped shallots to the bowl with the apples.

9. Mix to obtain a homogeneous mixture.
10. Take the pork loin and stuff it along the entire surface.
11. Roll up the meat on itself and seal the meat with kitchen twine.
12. Now put the white wine, mustard and two tablespoons of oil in a bowl and mix.
13. Brush the meat with the mustard emulsion.
14. Preheat the Pit Boss at 356 ° F for 10 minutes with the lid closed. Add some cherry chips to the smoked box.
15. Cook the pork loin indirectly for 1 hour with the lid closed.
16. Brush from time to time with the mustard emulsion.
17. After the hour, check the temperature and if it is 158 ° F then remove the roast from the grill. Otherwise, continue cooking until the temperature is reached.
18. Let it rest for 15 minutes, then cut the roast into slices and serve.

Tournedos

PREPARATION TIME: 20 minutes+1 night of marinating
COOKING TIME: 20 minutes
DIFFICULT LEVEL: Simple
CALORIES FOR 100 GRAMS: 300
FAT FOR 100 GRAMS: 2
CARBOIDRATES FOR 100 GRAMS: 12
PROTEINS FOR 100 GRAMS: 42

INGREDIENTS FOR 4 SERVINGS

- 1 pork filet mignon of 600 grams
- 500 ml of white wine
- 2 cloves of garlic
- 2 bay leaves
- 1 sprig of chopped parsley
- 50 ml of cooking cream
- 30 grams of grated Parmesan cheese
- Salt and pepper to taste
- Olive oil to taste

DIRECTIONS

1. Wash and dry the fillet, remove excess fat and the silver skin.
2. Put them in a baking dish and sprinkle them with salt and pepper.
3. Peel and wash the garlic cloves and then chop them.
4. Wash and dry the bay leaf.
5. Put garlic, bay leaf, olive oil in the bowl with the meat.
6. Sprinkle everything with the white wine, then cover the bowl and leave the meat to marinate in the fridge overnight.
7. Preheat the Pit Boss at 356 ° for 10 minutes with the lid closed.
8. Cook the fillet on direct cooking for 15 minutes with the lid closed.
9. Turn it every 5 minutes and brush it with the marinating liquid.
10. As soon as they are cooked, remove them from the barbecue

and let them rest for 10 minutes.

11. Meanwhile, prepare the sauce.
12. Put half of the marinating liquid in a saucepan.
13. Bring to a boil and then add the Parmesan and cream.
14. Stir, melt the cheese and turn off.
15. Cut the fillet into 1 cm thick slices and place them on plates.
16. Sprinkle with the cheese sauce and serve.

Pork fillet with sour cherries

PREPARATION TIME: 30 minutes
COOKING TIME: 25 minutes
DIFFICULT LEVEL: Simple
CALORIES FOR 100 GRAMS: 310
FAT FOR 100 GRAMS: 14
CARBOIDRATES FOR 100 GRAMS: 17
PROTEINS FOR 100 GRAMS: 25

INGREDIENTS FOR 4 SERVINGS
- 1 whole pork fillet of 400 grams
- 16 sour cherries in syrup
- 150 grams of sour cherry syrup
- 1 sprig of thyme
- 100 ml of white wine
- 2 sprigs of rosemary
- Salt flavoured with herbs to taste
- Olive oil to taste
- Pepper to taste

DIRECTIONS
1. Wash and dry sage, thyme and rosemary, then chop them.
2. Wash and dry the fillet, remove grease and silver skin and then brush it with olive oil.
3. Sprinkle the entire surface of the fillet with flavoured salt, pepper and the mix of aromatic herbs.
4. Preheat the Pit Boss at 338 ° F for 10 minutes.
5. Now place the fillet on the grill and cook for 15 minutes, or until the internal temperature is 149 ° F.
6. As soon as it is cooked, remove it from the grill and let it rest for 10 minutes.
7. Meanwhile, prepare the black cherry sauce.
8. Put the black cherries, the wine, 30 ml of water and the syrup in a saucepan.

9. Cook for 7 minutes, stirring constantly.
10. After 10 minutes, cut the fillet into slices.
11. Put the fillet on the plates, sprinkle with the sour cherry sauce and serve.

Loin with carrot cream and curry

PREPARATION TIME: 30 minutes + 1 hour of marinating
COOKING TIME: 20 minutes
DIFFICULT LEVEL: Simple
CALORIES FOR 100 GRAMS: 265
FAT FOR 100 GRAMS: 16
CARBOIDRATES FOR 100 GRAMS: 5
PROTEINS FOR 100 GRAMS: 23

INGREDIENTS FOR 4 SERVINGS

- 1 whole loin of 400 grams
- 2 carrots
- 200 ml of cooking cream
- 2 tablespoons of curry
- 100 ml of white wine
- 1 tablespoon of dried bay leaves
- 1 sprig of chopped parsley
- Olive oil to taste
- Salt and pepper to taste

DIRECTIONS

1. Remove excess fat and the silver skin from the loin.
2. Wash it, dry it and put it in a bowl.
3. Add salt, pepper, olive oil, dried bay leaf in the bowl, and then cover the bowl and leave to marinate for 1 hour.
4. In the meantime, peel the carrots, wash them and then put them to cook for 15 minutes in boiling water and salt.
5. Drain and set aside.
6. Preheat the Pit Boss at 392 ° F for 15 minutes.
7. Put the loin to cook for 20 minutes.
8. Check the temperature and if it is 149 ° F then remove the loin from the barbecue, otherwise continue until the temperature is reached.
9. Just cooked, remove the loin from the Pit Boss and let it rest for

10 minutes.

10. Heat a tablespoon of olive oil in a pan. Put the carrots cut into cubes and sauté them for 2 minutes.

11. Add the curry and cream. Mix, season with salt, pepper, and cook for 5 minutes.

12. Take an immersion blender and blend everything.

13. Now cut the loin into cubes. Put it in the pan with the carrot sauce and mix.

14. Now put the loin in the serving dishes and serve.

Pork stew with sweet and sour onions

PREPARATION TIME: 30 minutes
COOKING TIME: 60 minutes
DIFFICULT LEVEL: Medium
CALORIES FOR 100 GRAMS: 216
FAT FOR 100 GRAMS: 6
CARBOIDRATES FOR 100 GRAMS: 8
PROTEINS FOR 100 GRAMS: 22

INGREDIENTS FOR 4 SERVINGS
- 800 grams of pork loin
- 3 onions
- 2 apples
- 1 clove of garlic
- 1 tablespoon of brown sugar
- 200 ml of white wine
- 100 ml of balsamic vinegar
- 2 sprigs of rosemary
- 400 ml of meat broth
- Salt and pepper to taste
- Olive oil to taste

DIRECTIONS
1. Wash and dry the loin and then cut it into cubes.
2. Peel and wash the garlic and then chop it.
3. Peel and wash the apples, remove the seeds and then cut them into cubes.
4. Wash and dry the rosemary.
5. Peel the onions, wash them and cut them into slices.
6. Preheat the Pit Boss at 338 ° F for 15 minutes.
7. Now put a cast iron saucepan to heat for 10 minutes.
8. As soon as it is hot, put two tablespoons of olive oil to heat and then put the garlic to brown.
9. Add the cubes of loin, mix well and sauté for 3 minutes.

10. Now add the wine. Continue cooking, for another 2 minutes, always stirring.
11. Now add the apple cubes and rosemary. Season with salt, pepper, and cook for 10 minutes.
12. Now add the broth, put the lid on the saucepan and cook for another 45 minutes.
13. In the meantime, put a tablespoon of oil in a pan and let it heat up.
14. Put the onions, sugar and balsamic vinegar.
15. Cook for 15 minutes, stirring often.
16. As soon as the stew is cooked, remove it from the Pit Boss and let it rest for 5 minutes.
17. Put the onion in the saucepan with the meat and mix well.
18. Now put the stew on the plates and serve.

Pork belly with citrus fruits

PREPARATION TIME: 40 minutes+ 8 hours of marinating
COOKING TIME: 1hour and 30 minutes
DIFFICULT LEVEL: Medium
CALORIES FOR 100 GRAMS: 518
FAT FOR 100 GRAMS: 27
CARBOIDRATES FOR 100 GRAMS: 4
PROTEINS FOR 100 GRAMS: 10

INGREDIENTS FOR 4 SERVINGS
- 1 pound of pork belly
- 1 apple
- 1 onion
- 100 grams of brown sugar
- 120 ml of apple cider vinegar
- 1 star anise
- 1 tsp ground cinnamon
- 120 ml of orange juice
- 30 ml of lime juice
- the grated rind of an orange
- 150 ml of vegetable broth
- Salt and pepper to taste
- Olive oil to taste

DIRECTIONS
1. Wash and dry the pork belly.
2. Make cuts in the rind.
3. Brush it with oil and then sprinkle the entire surface with salt and pepper.
4. Peel and wash the onion and apple and then chop them.
5. Massage the surface of the meat with the onion and apple mix and place the meat inside a vacuum bag.
6. Put the orange and lime juice in a saucepan. Add the grated zest, sugar, anise, cinnamon, broth, and vinegar and cook until

the sugar has completely dissolved.

7. Put the sauce inside the bag, seal it and put it in the fridge to marinate for 8 hours.
8. After 8 hours, preheat the Pit Boss at 356 ° F for 15 minutes.
9. Put the pork belly in the rotisserie.
10. Remove the pork belly from the bag and pour the cooking juices into a bowl.
11. Place the spit on the rotisserie and place a container of water under the pork belly.
12. Roast the pork belly for 1and 30 minutes, until the internal temperature reaches 158 ° F, brushing with the marinating liquid from time to time.
13. Just cooked remove the belly from the Pit Boss and let it rest for 15 minutes.
14. In the meantime, strain the marinade in a saucepan and bring to a boil.
15. Cut the pork belly, put it on plates, sprinkle with the marinating liquid and serve.

Fruit salad with grilled pork loin

PREPARATION TIME: 30 minutes
COOKING TIME: 25 minutes
DIFFICULT LEVEL: Simple
CALORIES FOR 100 GRAMS: 189
FAT FOR 100 GRAMS: 6
CARBOIDRATES FOR 100 GRAMS: 11
PROTEINS FOR 100 GRAMS: 23

INGREDIENTS FOR 4 SERVINGS

- 1 pork loin of 500 grams
- 1 tablespoon of dried bay leaf
- 2 teaspoons of paprika
- 1 melon
- 12 strawberries
- 100 grams of mixed green salad
- 60 ml of sherry
- Apple cider vinegar to taste
- Salt and pepper to taste

DIRECTIONS

1. Wash and dry the pork loin.
2. In a bowl put the sherry, salt, pepper, bay leaf and paprika and mix well.
3. Brush the meat with oil and then cover it with the sherry mix.
4. Preheat the Pit Boss at 338 ° F for 15 minutes.
5. Place the loin on the grill and cook with the lid closed for 25 minutes, or until it has reached an internal temperature of 158 ° F.
6. Just cooked, remove it from the barbecue and let it rest for 15 minutes.
7. Meanwhile, peel the melon, remove the seeds and cut the pulp into cubes.
8. Wash and dry the strawberries and then cut them into slices.

9. Wash and dry the green salad.
10. Put the green salad first, then the melon and finally the strawberries on a serving dish.
11. Put the loin fillets on top and season with oil, salt, pepper, and apple cider vinegar.
12. Put on the table and serve.

Sweet and Sour Pork

PREPARATION TIME: 15 minutes
COOKING TIME: 20 minutes
DIFFICULT LEVEL: Simple
CALORIES FOR 100 GRAMS: 132
FAT FOR 100 GRAMS: 5
CARBOIDRATES FOR 100 GRAMS: 13
PROTEINS FOR 100 GRAMS: 13

INGREDIENTS FOR 4 SERVINGS
- 400 grams of pork loin
- 150 grams of pineapple pulp
- 1 carrot
- 1 shallot
- 2 red peppers
- 60 ml of balsamic vinegar
- 1 tablespoon of cornstarch
- 40 ml of soy sauce
- 100 grams of brown sugar
- 60 ml of pineapple juice
- 200 ml of tomato sauce
- Salt and pepper to taste
- Olive oil to taste

DIRECTIONS
1. Wash and dry the loin and then cut it into cubes.
2. Wash the peppers, remove the seeds and white filaments and then cut them into strips.
3. Cut the pineapple pulp into cubes.
4. Preheat the Pit Boss for 10 minutes at 356 ° F.
5. Place the barbecue wok on the grill and heat it for 10 minutes.
6. Put two tablespoons of olive oil in the wok and let it heat up.
7. Now add the pork and the peppers and sauté them for 3 minutes.

8. Now add the pineapple and mix. Cook for 5 minutes and then remove them from the wok and set aside.
9. Now put the tomato puree, vinegar, pineapple juice and soy sauce in the wok.
10. Bring to a boil and add the cornstarch, dissolved in a glass of cold water.
11. Let the sauce thicken and then put the pineapple, pork and peppers back inside.
12. Continue cooking for a couple of minutes and then remove the wok from the Pit Boss.
13. Let it rest for a couple of minutes, then put on plates and serve.

Pork rolls with bacon and pistachios

PREPARATION TIME: 15 minutes
COOKING TIME: 15 minutes
DIFFICULT LEVEL: Simple
CALORIES FOR 100 GRAMS: 172
FAT FOR 100 GRAMS: 16
CARBOIDRATES FOR 100 GRAMS: 2
PROTEINS FOR 100 GRAMS: 27

INGREDIENTS FOR 4 SERVINGS

- 12 slices of pork loin of 100 grams each
- 12 slices of bacon
- 50 grams of chopped pistachios
- 12 sage leaves
- 100 ml of wine
- Flour to taste
- Salt and pepper to taste
- Olive oil to taste

DIRECTIONS

1. Wash and dry the slices of loin.
2. Sprinkle them on both sides with salt and pepper.
3. Wash and dry the sage leaves.
4. Place a slice of bacon, a little chopped pistachios and a sage leaf on each slice.
5. Roll up the slices on themselves and keep them closed with kitchen twine.
6. Brush the meat with a mix of wine and olive oil and then pass them over the flour.
7. Pre-heat the Pit Boss to 338 ° F for 10 minutes.
8. Now put the rolls directly on the grill and cook them for 15 minutes, turning them continuously and brushing them with a little oil.
9. As soon as they are cooked, remove them from the grill and let

them rest for 5 minutes.

10. Remove the string, put the rolls on plates and serve.

Canadian bacon

PREPARATION TIME: 20 minutes+ 4 days of marinating
COOKING TIME: 1 hour and 30 minutes
DIFFICULT LEVEL: Medium
CALORIES FOR 100 GRAMS: 186
FAT FOR 100 GRAMS: 8
CARBOIDRATES FOR 100 GRAMS: 15
PROTEINS FOR 100 GRAMS: 12

INGREDIENTS FOR 4 SERVINGS

- 1 whole pork loin of 800 grams
- 4 litres of water
- 200 grams of brown sugar
- 100 ml of maple syrup
- 3 cloves of garlic
- 2 tablespoons of dried thyme
- 2 tablespoons of dried sage
- 1 tablespoon of paprika
- Salt and pepper to taste
- Olive oil to taste

DIRECTIONS

1. Start by removing excess fat and silver skins from the loin.
2. Wash it and dry it.
3. Peel and wash the garlic and then chop it.
4. In a saucepan, pour the water, brown sugar, maple syrup, garlic, thyme, sage, paprika, salt and pepper.
5. Stir and cook until the salt and sugar have completely dissolved, then turn off the heat and let it cool.
6. Put the meat in a vacuum bag, add the brine, suck in the air and then seal it.
7. Leave the meat to rest in the fridge for 72 hours.
8. After 72 hours, take the meat, rinse it under running water, and then dab with absorbent paper.

9. Put the meat back in the fridge to rest for another 24 hours.
10. After 24 hours, preheat the Pit Boss for 15 minutes at 230 ° F.
11. Add apple chips to the smoked box.
12. Put the loin in the barbecue and cook with the lid closed for 1 hour and 30. Check the internal temperature and if it has not yet reached 158 ° F continue cooking until the temperature is reached.
13. As soon as it is cooked, remove the Canadian bacon from the grill; brush a light veil of oil over the entire surface.
14. Let cool completely before slicing and serving.

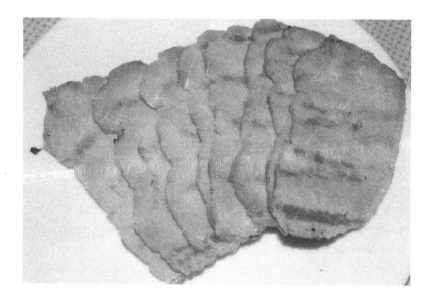

Pork ribs in vinegar

PREPARATION TIME: 30 minutes
COOKING TIME: 45 minutes
DIFFICULT LEVEL: Simple
CALORIES FOR 100 GRAMS: 193
FAT FOR 100 GRAMS: 13
CARBOIDRATES FOR 100 GRAMS: 5
PROTEINS FOR 100 GRAMS: 17

INGREDIENTS FOR 4 SERVINGS

- 8 pork ribs of 100 grams each
- 4 shallots
- 2 cloves of garlic
- 2 sprigs of thyme
- 100 ml of balsamic vinegar
- Olive oil to taste
- Salt and pepper to taste

DIRECTIONS

1. Preheat the Pit Boss at 356 ° F for 15 minutes with the lid closed.
2. Wash and dry the ribs, brush them with oil, sprinkle them with salt and pepper, and then put them in a roasting pan.
3. Peel and wash the sausages, cut them into slices and put them in the roasting pan with the meat.
4. Wash and dry the thyme and put it in size.
5. Put the balsamic vinegar in the cutter and then cover the pan with a sheet of aluminium foil.
6. Place the roasting pan with the ribs on the grill and cook with the lid closed for 45 minutes.
7. Just cooked, remove them from the barbecue and let them rest for 15 minutes.
8. After 10 minutes, remove the aluminium foil and put the ribs on the plates.
9. Garnish with the shallots, sprinkle with the cooking juices and serve.

Pork loin with myrtle

PREPARATION TIME: 20 minutes
COOKING TIME: 60 minutes
DIFFICULT LEVEL: Simple
CALORIES FOR 100 GRAMS: 158
FAT FOR 100 GRAMS: 6
CARBOIDRATES FOR 100 GRAMS: 2
PROTEINS FOR 100 GRAMS: 19

INGREDIENTS FOR 4 SERVINGS

- 800 grams of pork loin
- 100 ml of white wine
- 10 tangerines
- 100 grams of sliced speck
- 4 sprigs of myrtle
- Salt and pepper to taste
- Olive oil to taste

DIRECTIONS

1. Preheat the Pit Boss at 356 ° for 15 minutes with the lid closed.
2. Wash and dry the loin, remove the excess fat and the silver skin.
3. Wash and dry the myrtle sprigs.
4. Brush the meat with olive oil and sprinkle the entire surface with pepper and a little salt.
5. Now wrap the loin with the slices of speck and wrap the meat with cooking string.
6. Now put the loin in a roasting pan and pour in the white wine.
7. Squeeze the mandarins and strain the juice into the roasting pan with the pork.
8. Finally add the sprigs of myrtle and place the roasting pan on the grill.
9. Close the lid and cook the loin for 60 minutes, or until the core temperature of the meat reaches 158 ° F.
10. Just cooked, remove the loin from the Pit Boss and let it rest for

15 minutes.

11. Now cut the meat into slices, put it on plates, sprinkle with the cooking juices and serve.

Pork knuckle with beer

PREPARATION TIME: 20 minutes+ 3hours of marinating
COOKING TIME: 2 hours and 30 minutes
DIFFICULT LEVEL: Simple
CALORIES FOR 100 GRAMS: 240
FAT FOR 100 GRAMS: 16
CARBOIDRATES FOR 100 GRAMS: 1
PROTEINS FOR 100 GRAMS: 15

INGREDIENTS FOR 4 SERVINGS

- 1 kilo pork knuckle
- 2 tablespoons of chopped thyme
- 1 tsp ground cinnamon
- 1 tablespoon of chopped rosemary
- 1 minced clove of garlic
- 500 ml of light beer
- 1 teaspoon of nutmeg
- Salt and pepper to taste
- Olive oil to taste

DIRECTIONS

1. Wash and dry the pork knuckle and then put it in a bowl.
2. Sprinkle it with salt and then pour the beer.
3. Cover the bowl and put to marinate in the fridge for 3 hours.
4. After 3 hours, remove it from the fridge.
5. Preheat the Pit Boss at 302 ° F for 15 minutes.
6. Add whiskey and cherry chips to the smoked box.
7. Put thyme, garlic, rosemary, salt, pepper, cinnamon, nutmeg, and 3 tablespoons of olive oil in a bowl and mix well.
8. Take the knuckle and sprinkle the entire surface with the rub.
9. Place the knuckle on the grill in the middle. Close the lid and cook for 2 hours.
10. Remove it from the grill and wrap the knuckle with aluminium foil.

11. Continue cooking for another 30 minutes or until the core temperature of the meat has reached 208 ° F.
12. As soon as it is ready, remove it from the Pit Boss and let it rest for 1 hour.
13. After the hour, remove the knuckle from the aluminium foil, slice it, put it on plates and serve.

Pork chops with pears and pumpkin

PREPARATION TIME: 20 minutes +3 hours of marinating
COOKING TIME: 20 minutes
DIFFICULT LEVEL: Simple
CALORIES FOR 100 GRAMS: 321
FAT FOR 100 GRAMS: 14
CARBOIDRATES FOR 100 GRAMS: 18
PROTEINS FOR 100 GRAMS: 31

INGREDIENTS FOR 4 SERVINGS

- 4 pork chops of 150 grams each
- 1 onion
- 1 lemon
- 6 sage leaves
- 300 grams of pumpkin pulp
- 2 pears
- 150 ml of white wine
- Salt and pepper to taste
- Olive oil to taste

DIRECTIONS

1. Wash and dry the pork chops and then put them in a baking dish.
2. Sprinkle them with salt and pepper.
3. Wash and dry the sage and put it in the bowl with the chops.
4. Add the wine, 3 tablespoons of olive oil and the filtered lemon juice.
5. Cover the pan and marinate for 3 hours.
6. In the meantime, wash and dry the pumpkin and cut it into cubes.
7. Wash the pears, remove the stalk and the seeds and then cut them into slices.
8. Peel and wash the onion and then chop it.
9. Remove the chops from the fridge.

10. Preheat the Pit Boss at 374 ° F for 10 minutes.
11. Now put the chops on direct heat and cook them for 10 minutes, with the lid closed and turning them only once.
12. As soon as the internal temperature of the meat has reached 149 ° F, remove them from the Pit Boss and let them rest for 5 minutes.
13. Take a pan and heat 1 tablespoon of olive oil.
14. As soon as it is hot, put the onion to brown.
15. Put the pumpkin, season with salt and pepper and add a glass of water.
16. Cook for 10 minutes and then add the pears.
17. Continue cooking for another 5 minutes, then put the chops in the pan and let them cook for 1 minute.
18. Put the meat on the plates and add the pumpkin and pear.
19. Sprinkle with the cooking juices and serve.

Black tea smoked loin

PREPARATION TIME: 15 minutes
COOKING TIME: 1 hour
DIFFICULT LEVEL: Simple
CALORIES FOR 100 GRAMS: 153
FAT FOR 100 GRAMS: 6
CARBOIDRATES FOR 100 GRAMS: 1
PROTEINS FOR 100 GRAMS: 21

INGREDIENTS FOR 4 SERVINGS

- 1.2-pound pork loin
- 1 clove of garlic
- 4 bay leaves
- 4 juniper berries
- 1 sprig of rosemary
- 4 tablespoons of black tea
- Salt and pepper to taste
- Olive oil to taste

DIRECTIONS

1. Wash and dry the loin. Remove excess fat and silver skin.
2. Wash and dry the bay leaves and rosemary and then chop them.
3. Peel and wash the garlic and then chop it.
4. In a bowl mix together bay leaves, rosemary, salt, pepper and black tea.
5. Brush the loin with olive oil and then sprinkle it with the rub, making sure that it adheres well to the entire surface of the meat.
6. Preheat the Pit Boss at 230 ° F for 10 minutes.
7. Put a handful of hickory chips and a cherry in the smoker box.
8. Put the loin on direct heat and close the lid.
9. Cook for an hour or until the core temperature of the meat reaches 149 ° F.
10. Now remove the loin from the grill and let it rest for 10 minutes wrapped in aluminium foil.

11. After 10 minutes remove the meat from the aluminium foil, cut into slices, put on serving plates and serve.

Smoked pork fillet with coffee and brown sugar

PREPARATION TIME: 20 minutes
COOKING TIME: 35 minutes
DIFFICULT LEVEL: Simple
CALORIES FOR 100 GRAMS: 153
FAT FOR 100 GRAMS: 6
CARBOIDRATES FOR 100 GRAMS: 1
PROTEINS FOR 100 GRAMS: 21

INGREDIENTS FOR 4 SERVINGS
- 800 grams of pork tenderloin
- 1 tablespoon of ground coffee
- 1 tablespoon of smoked paprika
- 50 ml of white wine
- 1 teaspoon of cumin
- 1 tablespoon of brown sugar
- Salt and pepper to taste
- Olive oil to taste

DIRECTIONS
1. Wash and dry the fillet and remove excess fat.
2. In a bowl put the coffee, paprika, sugar, salt and pepper and mix well.
3. Brush the meat first with wine and then with olive oil.
4. Now sprinkle the entire surface with the mix of spices and coffee.
5. Preheat the Pit Boss at 266 ° F for 15 minutes.
6. Put a handful of apple chips in the smoked box.
7. Put the fillet to cook for 35 minutes, or until the core temperature of the meat, reaches 158 ° F.
8. As soon as it is cooked, remove the fillet from the barbecue and let it rest for 5 minutes.
9. Cut it into slices, put it on serving plates and serve with sauce of your choice.

Pork stew with plums

PREPARATION TIME: 30 minutes
COOKING TIME: 60 minutes
DIFFICULT LEVEL: Simple
CALORIES FOR 100 GRAMS: 268
FAT FOR 100 GRAMS: 10
CARBOIDRATES FOR 100 GRAMS: 18
PROTEINS FOR 100 GRAMS: 23

INGREDIENTS FOR 4 SERVINGS
- 1 pork fillet of 800 grams
- 4 spring onions
- 200 ml of plum liqueur
- 6 plums
- 2 bay leaves
- 100 ml of white wine
- 200 ml of meat broth
- Flour to taste
- Salt and pepper to taste
- Olive oil to taste

DIRECTIONS
1. Remove the excess fat from the meat.
2. Wash and dry it and then cut it into cubes.
3. Put the flour on a plate and then flour the meat cubes.
4. Wash the spring onions and then cut them into slices.
5. Wash the plums, cut them in half and remove the stone.
6. Wash and dry the bay leaves.
7. Preheat the Pit Boss at 338 ° F for 15 minutes.
8. Put a cast iron saucepan on the grill and let it heat for 10 minutes, over direct heat.
9. After 10 minutes, put two tablespoons of oil to heat in the saucepan.
10. Now add the bay leaves and the meat and sauté for 3 minutes.

11. Now add the wine and let it evaporate.
12. Season with salt and pepper and put the spring onions.
13. Now add the plum liqueur, the meat broth and put the lid on the saucepan.
14. Cook for 30 minutes, and then add the prunes.
15. Continue cooking for another 10 minutes.
16. As soon as it is cooked, remove the saucepan from the barbecue and let it rest for 5 minutes.
17. Remove the bay leaves, put the stew on the plates and serve.

Leg of pork in cider

PREPARATION TIME: 20 minutes+8 hours of marinating
COOKING TIME: 2 hours and 30 minutes
DIFFICULT LEVEL: Simple
CALORIES FOR 100 GRAMS: 273
FAT FOR 100 GRAMS: 17
CARBOIDRATES FOR 100 GRAMS: 1
PROTEINS FOR 100 GRAMS: 26

INGREDIENTS FOR 8 SERVINGS

- a 2-pound leg of pork
- 300 ml of cider
- a teaspoon of ground cloves
- 2 small pieces of ginger powder
- 2 tsp ground cinnamon
- Salt and pepper to taste
- Olive oil to taste

DIRECTIONS

1. Wash and dry the leg of pork and then cut the rind into diamond shapes.
2. Put it in a large bowl and sprinkle it with the cider.
3. Cover the bowl and place in the fridge to marinate for 8 hours.
4. After 8 hours, remove the meat from the fridge.
5. In a bowl mix together the spices, salt and pepper.
6. Brush the surface of the leg with olive oil and then sprinkle the entire surface of the meat with the rub.
7. Preheat the Pit Boss at 302 ° F for 15 minutes with the lid closed.
8. Put the leg of pork on the spit and then mount the spit in the rotisserie.
9. Cook for 30 minutes and then brush the meat with the marinating liquid.
10. Cook for another 2 hours, brushing the meat every 30 minutes.

11. As soon as the internal temperature of the meat reaches 185 ° F, remove the meat from the spit and let it rest in the heat for 15 minutes.
12. Put the leg in a serving dish and slice it directly on the table.

Pork chops with red and black salt

PREPARATION TIME: 20 minutes
COOKING TIME: 20 minutes
DIFFICULT LEVEL: Simple
CALORIES FOR 100 GRAMS: 288
FAT FOR 100 GRAMS: 21
CARBOIDRATES FOR 100 GRAMS: 2
PROTEINS FOR 100 GRAMS: 21

INGREDIENTS FOR 4 SERVINGS
- 4 pork chops of 150 grams each
- 1 clove of garlic
- 2 sprigs of chopped parsley
- 1 tablespoon of thyme leaves
- 2 teaspoons of red Hawaiian salt
- 1 teaspoon of smoked paprika
- 2 teaspoons of black Hawaiian salt
- Salt and pepper to taste
- Olive oil to taste

DIRECTIONS
1. Wash and dry the pork chops.
2. In a bowl mix together salt, pepper, paprika, red salt, black salt, parsley and thyme.
3. Brush the chops with olive oil and then sprinkle them along the entire surface with the salt rub.
4. Preheat the Pit Boss at 374 ° F for 15 minutes.
5. Place the chops on the grill and cook for 5 minutes on each side, with the lid closed.
6. As soon as they are cooked, remove them from the Pit Boss and let them rest for 10 minutes.
7. Meanwhile, wash the pumpkin and then cut it into cubes.
8. Peel and wash the garlic and then chop it.
9. Heat a little oil in the pan and brown the garlic.

10. Put the pumpkin pulp to brown for 10 minutes. Season with salt and pepper and turn off.
11. Put the chops on plates, garnish with the pumpkin and serve.

Pork chops with Mexican marinade

PREPARATION TIME: 15 minutes+2 hours of marinating
COOKING TIME: 80 minutes
DIFFICULT LEVEL: Simple
CALORIES FOR 100 GRAMS: 289
FAT FOR 100 GRAMS: 21
CARBOIDRATES FOR 100 GRAMS: 2
PROTEINS FOR 100 GRAMS: 21

INGREDIENTS FOR 4 SERVINGS
- 1 pound of pork ribs
- 1 tablespoon of onion powder
- 2 teaspoons of dried oregano
- 2 chopped chillies
- 1 teaspoon of garlic powder
- 2 teaspoons of cumin
- Olive oil to taste
- Salt and pepper to taste

DIRECTIONS
1. In a bowl mix together the onion, oregano, chopped chilli, garlic, cumin, salt and pepper.
2. Wash and dry the ribs and then brush them with olive oil.
3. Put the chops in a baking dish and sprinkle them on both sides with the rub.
4. Cover the bowl with cling film and leave to marinate for 2 hours.
5. After 2 hours, preheat the Pit Boss at 356 ° F for 15 minutes with the lid closed.
6. Cook the ribs with the bones facing downwards, with the lid closed, until the surface of the meat is dry and browned. It will take more or less 4 minutes.
7. Now remove the chops and wrap them in aluminium foil.

8. Return to the barbecue and continue cooking for another 40 minutes or until they have reached the core temperature of 194 ° F.
9. Just cooked, let the ribs rest for 10 minutes and then remove the aluminium foil.
10. Now slice the ribs, put them on plates and serve.

Pork chops with honey, balsamic vinegar and mustard

PREPARATION TIME: 15 minute + 2 hour of marinating
COOKING TIME: 8 minutes
DIFFICULT LEVEL: Simple
CALORIES FOR 100 GRAMS: 391
FAT FOR 100 GRAMS: 22
CARBOIDRATES FOR 100 GRAMS: 4
PROTEINS FOR 100 GRAMS: 23

INGREDIENTS FOR 4 SERVINGS

- 8 pork chops of 100 grams each
- 4 tablespoons of ketchup
- 60 ml of soy sauce
- 120 grams of honey
- 120 grams of mustard
- 120 ml of balsamic vinegar
- 20 grams of grated ginger
- Salt and pepper to taste
- Olive oil taste

DIRECTIONS

1. Put all the ingredients, except the meat, in a bowl and mix everything well.
2. Wash and dry the pork chops and then put them in the bowl.
3. Cover the bowl with cling film and then put in the fridge to marinate for 2 hours.
4. After 2 hours, remove the meat from the fridge.
5. Preheat the Pit Boss at 374 ° F for 15 minutes.
6. Place the pork chops on the grill and cook for 4 minutes on the side, with the lid closed.
7. As soon as they are cooked, remove them from the barbecue and let them rest for 10 minutes.
8. In the meantime, add the marinating liquid and let it reduce for 10 minutes.
9. Put the chops on plates, sprinkle with the marinating liquid and serve.

Roast pork with hazelnuts

PREPARATION TIME: 20 minutes
COOKING TIME: 60 minutes
DIFFICULT LEVEL: Simple
CALORIES FOR 100 GRAMS: 257
FAT FOR 100 GRAMS: 16
CARBOIDRATES FOR 100 GRAMS: 2
PROTEINS FOR 100 GRAMS: 27

INGREDIENTS FOR 4 SERVINGS
- 800 grams of pork loin
- half onion
- 1 small carrot
- 1 clove of garlic
- 1 sprig of rosemary
- 2 bay leaves
- 4 sage leaves
- 4 juniper berries
- 100 ml of white wine
- 15 grams of hazelnuts
- Olive oil to taste
- Salt and pepper to taste

DIRECTIONS
1. Wash and dry the pork loin and remove the excess fat.
2. Brush the meat with olive oil and sprinkle the meat with salt and pepper.
3. Put the loin in a roasting pan.
4. Peel and wash the carrot and onion and then chop them.
5. Wash and dry the rosemary, bay leaf and sage.
6. Put the onion and carrot, aromatic herbs and juniper berries in the roasting pan.
7. Sprinkle now with white wine.
8. Preheat the Pit Boss at 356 ° F for 15 minutes.

9. Place the roasting pan on the grill, close the lid and cook for 60 minutes, or until the core temperature of the meat, reaches 158 ° F.
10. Just cooked, remove the roast from the Pit Boss and let it rest for 10 minutes.
11. Cut the roast into slices and place them on serving plates.
12. Put the cooking juices in the glass of the mixer together with two tablespoons of olive oil and the hazelnuts.
13. Operate the mixer and chop until you get a smooth and homogeneous cream.
14. Sprinkle the roast with the hazelnut sauce and serve.

Stuffed pork belly

PREPARATION TIME: 30 minutes+8 hours of marinating
COOKING TIME: 1 hour and 30 minutes
DIFFICULT LEVEL: Medium
CALORIES FOR 100 GRAMS: 548
FAT FOR 100 GRAMS: 43
CARBOIDRATES FOR 100 GRAMS: 2
PROTEINS FOR 100 GRAMS: 35

INGREDIENTS FOR 6 SERVINGS
- 1.2 pounds of pork belly
- 2 red peppers
- 300 grams of mushrooms
- 2 cloves of garlic
- 1 lemon
- 100 grams of breadcrumbs
- 2 sprigs of dill
- Olive oil to taste
- Salt and pepper to taste

DIRECTIONS
1. Wash and dry the pork belly, remove the excess fat and the silver skin.
2. Cut the belly in two halves.
3. Squeeze the lemon juice, then brush the entire surface of the meat with the juice, and then sprinkle it with salt and pepper.
4. Put the meat in a bowl, close it and let it marinate for 8 hours.
5. After the marinating time, remove the meat from the fridge and let it rest at room temperature until ready for use.
6. Wash and dry the mushrooms and then cut them into slices.
7. Wash the peppers, remove the seeds and then cut them into cubes.
8. Peel and wash the garlic and then chop them.
9. Put a spoonful of olive oil in a pan and then put the garlic to

brown.

10. Add the mushrooms, mix, and season with salt, pepper, and cook for 4 minutes. Add the peppers and continue cooking for another 6 minutes.
11. Put the mushrooms and peppers in a bowl and add the breadcrumbs and the dill cut into small pieces.
12. Mix everything well.
13. Now put the filling inside the pork belly and then close it and wrap it with kitchen twine.
14. Now preheat the Pit Boss at 365 ° F for 15 minutes.
15. Put the pork belly in a roasting pan on a roasting pan.
16. Place the roasting pan in the Pit Boss and cook for 1 hour and 30 minutes, or until the core temperature of the meat, reaches 158 ° F.
17. Just cooked remove the belly from the Pit Boss and let it rest for 15 minutes.
18. Now cut the belly into slices put on plates and serve.

Pork stew with black olives

PREPARATION TIME: 15 minutes
COOKING TIME: 60 minutes
DIFFICULT LEVEL: Simple
CALORIES FOR 100 GRAMS: 218
FAT FOR 100 GRAMS: 11
CARBOIDRATES FOR 100 GRAMS: 11
PROTEINS FOR 100 GRAMS: 21

INGREDIENTS FOR 4 SERVINGS

- 600 grams of pork loin
- 150 grams of tomato pulp
- 20 black olives
- 1 clove of garlic
- 2 sage leaves
- 4 juniper berries
- Salt and pepper to taste
- Olive oil to taste

DIRECTIONS

1. Wash and dry the pork loin then cut it into cubes.
2. Peel and wash the garlic and then chop it.
3. Preheat the Pit Boss at 356 ° F for 15 minutes with the lid closed.
4. Preheat a cast iron saucepan for 10 minutes.
5. Put two tablespoons of oil in the saucepan and then put the garlic to brown.
6. Add the meat and brown it for 4 minutes.
7. Now add the tomato pulp, season with salt and pepper and mix.
8. Cook for 5 minutes and then add two glasses of water.
9. Close the saucepan with the lid and cook for 45 minutes, stirring occasionally.
10. Now add the olives, stir and continue cooking for another 5 minutes.
11. Remove from the Pit Boss and let it sit for 5 minutes.
12. Now put the stew on the plates and serve.

Pork tenderloin with truffle sauce

PREPARATION TIME: 25 minutes
COOKING TIME: 35 minutes
DIFFICULT LEVEL: Medium
CALORIES FOR 100 GRAMS: 180
FAT FOR 100 GRAMS: 10
CARBOIDRATES FOR 100 GRAMS: 7
PROTEINS FOR 100 GRAMS: 23

INGREDIENTS FOR 4 SERVINGS

- 800 grams of pork tenderloin
- 25 grams of black truffle
- 20 grams of butter
- 150 grams of fresh cheese
- 30 grams of grated Parmesan cheese
- 1 tablespoon of smoked paprika
- 1 tablespoon of dried bay leaf
- Salt and pepper to taste
- Olive oil to taste

DIRECTIONS

1. Start by removing the excess fat from the fillet, then wash and dry it.
2. Brush the fillet with olive oil, then sprinkle the entire surface with salt, pepper, paprika and bay leaf.
3. Preheat the Pit Boss at 248 ° F for 15 minutes.
4. Add a handful of apple chips to the smoke box.
5. Cook the fillet with the lid closed until it reaches 158 ° F at the heart. it will take about 35 minutes.
6. Just cooked, remove the fillet from the Pit Boss and let it rest for 10 minutes.
7. In the meantime, prepare the sauce.
8. Put the butter in a saucepan and let it melt.
9. Put the fresh cheese and stir until the cheese becomes liquid.

Add the parmesan and grated truffle and mix. Cook for a couple of minutes, season with salt and pepper and turn off.

10. Cut the fillet into slices. Sprinkle with the truffle sauce and serve.

Braised pork belly

PREPARATION TIME: 15 minutes
COOKING TIME: 70 minutes
DIFFICULT LEVEL: Medium
CALORIES FOR 100 GRAMS: 541
FAT FOR 100 GRAMS: 41
CARBOIDRATES FOR 100 GRAMS: 3
PROTEINS FOR 100 GRAMS: 37

INGREDIENTS FOR 4 SERVINGS

- 600 grams of pork belly
- 1 litre of meat broth
- 200 ml of red wine
- 1 onion
- 60 grams of dried plums
- Salt and pepper to taste
- Olive oil to taste

DIRECTIONS

1. Wash and dry the pork belly and then cut it into slices.
2. Preheat the Pit Boss at 302 ° F for 15 minutes with the lid closed.
3. Add some hickory chips to the smoke box.
4. Heat the barbecue wok for 10 minutes.
5. As soon as it is hot, put two tablespoons of olive oil to heat.
6. Peel and wash the onion and then chop it.
7. Put it in the wok and let it brown.
8. As soon as the onion is golden brown, brown on all sides for 5 minutes.
9. Now add the pitted plums and continue cooking for another 5 minutes.
10. Season with salt and pepper and add the wine.
11. Let it evaporate and finally add the broth.
12. Close the lid and cook for 1 hour, stirring occasionally.
13. Just cooked, remove the pork belly from the Pit Boss and let it

rest for 5 minutes.

14. Put the pork belly on plates, sprinkle with the cooking juices and serve.

Pork meatballs with orange cooked in the barbecue

PREPARATION TIME: 20 minutes
COOKING TIME: 10 minutes
DIFFICULT LEVEL: Simple
CALORIES FOR 100 GRAMS: 240
FAT FOR 100 GRAMS: 7
CARBOIDRATES FOR 100 GRAMS: 3
PROTEINS FOR 100 GRAMS: 18

INGREDIENTS FOR 4 SERVINGS
- 600 grams of minced pork
- 1 egg
- 40 grams of breadcrumbs
- 30 grams of grated Parmesan cheese
- 1 orange
- 1 shallot
- Flour to taste
- Olive oil to taste
- Salt and pepper to taste

DIRECTIONS
1. Put the minced meat in a bowl.
2. Add salt, pepper, egg, breadcrumbs and parmesan and mix well.
3. Wash and dry the orange and grate the zest inside the bowl with the meat.
4. Mix again and when you have obtained a homogeneous mixture, start forming the meatballs.
5. Put the flour on a plate and then flour the meatballs.
6. Preheat the Pit Boss at 356 ° F for 10 minutes.
7. Place a sheet of parchment paper on the grill and place the meatballs on top.
8. Close the lid and cook, indirectly for 10 minutes, turning the meatballs a couple of times.

9. Remove the meatballs from the Pit Boss, put them on the plates and serve immediately.

Indonesian pork skewers

PREPARATION TIME: 20 minutes+ 2 hours of marinating
COOKING TIME: 16 minutes
DIFFICULT LEVEL: Simple
CALORIES FOR 100 GRAMS: 199
FAT FOR 100 GRAMS: 14
CARBOIDRATES FOR 100 GRAMS: 4
PROTEINS FOR 100 GRAMS: 20

INGREDIENTS FOR 6 SERVINGS
- 750 of pork loin
- 300 ml of coconut milk
- 6 spring onions
- 2 stalks of lemon grass
- 2 hot peppers
- 2 cloves of garlic
- 1 teaspoon of grated ginger
- 1 lime
- 1 tablespoon of honey
- 40 ml of soy sauce
- Olive oil to taste

DIRECTIONS
1. Take a large enough bowl and pour the coconut milk.
2. Add the finely chopped chillies. Wash and dry the spring onions and chop only the white part. Add the spring onions inside the bowl.
3. Peel and wash the garlic cloves and then add them to the bowl.
4. Wash and dry the lime and then chop the zest and place it in the bowl.
5. Then pour in the soy sauce, ginger and honey.
6. Squeeze the lime and pour the juice into the bowl.
7. Cut the lemon grass stems into small pieces and add them to the marinade. Mix everything well with a fork.

8. Wash and dry the pork loin and then cut it into cubes.
9. Now put the meat in the bowl with the marinade, cover the bowl and put it in the fridge to marinate for 2 hours.
10. After two hours, remove the meat from the fridge.
11. Preheat the Pit Boss at 356 ° F for 15 minutes.
12. Put the meat cubes on the metal skewers and after 15 minutes, put them directly on the grill.
13. Cook for 4 minutes on each side, then remove from the grill and let it rest for 10 minutes.
14. In the meantime, put the marinating liquid in a saucepan.
15. Bring to a boil and then let the sauce thicken for 5 minutes.
16. Put the skewers on the plates, sprinkle with the sauce and serve.

Pork meatloaf

PREPARATION TIME: 20 minutes
COOKING TIME: 30 minutes
DIFFICULT LEVEL: Simple
CALORIES FOR 100 GRAMS: 191
FAT FOR 100 GRAMS: 11
CARBOIDRATES FOR 100 GRAMS: 7
PROTEINS FOR 100 GRAMS: 17

INGREDIENTS FOR 6 SERVINGS
- 600 grams of minced pork
- 2 eggs
- 100 grams of breadcrumbs
- 100 grams of grated Parmesan cheese
- 150 grams of smoked cheese
- Salt and pepper to taste
- Olive oil to taste

DIRECTIONS
1. In a bowl put the breadcrumbs, minced meat, eggs, grated Parmesan, salt and pepper.
2. Start mixing everything with a spoon and then continue with your hands to form a homogeneous and compact mixture.
3. Also, add the cubes of smoked cheese, give the meatloaf the classic rectangular shape, and compact the ends well.
4. Brush a sheet of aluminium foil and then put the meatloaf inside.
5. Seal the aluminium foil well.
6. Preheat the Pit Boss at 356 ° F for 15 minutes.
7. Put the meatloaf inside the Pit Boss, and cook for 30 minutes, with the lid closed.
8. Just cooked, remove the meatloaf from the barbecue and let it rest for about ten minutes.
9. After 10 minutes, open the aluminium foil, cut the meatloaf into slices and serve.

Japanese-style braised pork

PREPARATION TIME: 20 minutes
COOKING TIME: 2 hours
DIFFICULT LEVEL: Medium
CALORIES FOR 100 GRAMS: 255
FAT FOR 100 GRAMS: 15
CARBOIDRATES FOR 100 GRAMS: 4
PROTEINS FOR 100 GRAMS: 19

INGREDIENTS FOR 6 SERVINGS
- 800 grams of pork belly
- 3 tablespoons of brown sugar
- 1 shallot
- 2 tsp ground ginger
- 50 ml of sake
- 50 ml of soy sauce
- 3-star anise
- Salt and pepper to taste
- Olive oil to taste

DIRECTIONS
1. Wash and dry the pork belly and then cut it into cubes.
2. Preheat the Pit Boss at 266 ° F for 15 minutes and adding a mix of hickory and cherry chips in the smoke box.
3. Heat a barbecue wok for 10 minutes.
4. Put two tablespoons of oil inside and as soon as it is hot, put the pork belly to brown for 5 minutes.
5. Add the sugar and salt and let it caramelize.
6. Peel the shallot, wash it and then cut it into slices.
7. Add the shallot, ginger, soy sauce, star anise, 300 ml of water and sake.
8. Mix, season with salt, pepper, and close the lid of the Pit Boss.
9. Cook for 2 hours, adding chips from time to time in the smoke box.

10. Just cooked, remove the pork from the Pit Boss and let it rest for 5 minutes.
11. Put the pork belly on plates, sprinkle with the cooking juices and serve.

Red curry with pork

PREPARATION TIME: 20 minutes
COOKING TIME: 20 minutes
DIFFICULT LEVEL: Medium
CALORIES FOR 100 GRAMS: 218
FAT FOR 100 GRAMS: 7
CARBOIDRATES FOR 100 GRAMS: 4
PROTEINS FOR 100 GRAMS: 21

INGREDIENTS FOR 4 SERVINGS

- 500 grams of pork loin
- 500 ml of coconut milk
- 4 lime leaves
- 4 Thai red chillies
- 4 cloves of garlic
- 1 tablespoon of fish sauce
- 1 sprig of lemon grass
- 1 tablespoon of palm sugar
- 1 tablespoon of shrimp sauce

DIRECTIONS

1. Prepare the curry paste: soak the Thai peppers in warm water for 20 minutes
2. Peel and wash the garlic cloves and then chop them.
3. Wash and chop the lemongrass.
4. Drain the Thai peppers and then chop them.
5. Put everything in a bowl and add the shrimp sauce. Mix until you get a homogeneous mixture.
6. Wash and dry the meat and then cut it into slices.
7. Preheat the Pit Boss at 356 ° F for 10 minutes.
8. Scale a barbecue wok for 10 minutes.
9. Put the coconut milk in the wok and bring to a boil.
10. Add the curry paste and mix the ingredients.
11. Add the meat, a tablespoon of fish sauce and the sugar. Stir and

let cook for 5 minutes.

12. Wash the lemon leaves and put them in the wok.

13. Continue cooking for another 10 minutes and then remove the wok from the Pit Boss.

14. Put the meat, curry on the plates, and serve immediately.

Pork stew with peas

PREPARATION TIME: 20 minutes
COOKING TIME: 60 minutes
DIFFICULT LEVEL: Simple
CALORIES FOR 100 GRAMS: 211
FAT FOR 100 GRAMS: 7
CARBOIDRATES FOR 100 GRAMS: 7
PROTEINS FOR 100 GRAMS: 25

INGREDIENTS FOR 4 SERVINGS

- 700 grams of pork loin
- 1 kg of peas
- 1 onion
- 250 grams of tomato pulp
- 100 ml of red wine
- Olive oil to taste
- Salt and pepper to taste

DIRECTIONS

1. Preheat the Pit Boss at 374 ° F for 15 minutes, with the lid closed.
2. Heat a cast iron saucepan for 10 minutes.
3. Meanwhile, wash the pork and cut it into cubes.
4. Wash the peas and let them drain.
5. Peel the onion, wash it and chop it.
6. As soon as the saucepan has heated up, put two tablespoons of oil to heat.
7. Add the onion and brown it for a couple of minutes.
8. Now add the meat and brown it for 5 minutes, stirring often.
9. Season with salt and pepper and then add the red wine.
10. Let the wine evaporate and then add the tomato and peas.
11. Add two glasses of water stir and close the saucepan with the lid.
12. Cook for 60 minutes, season with salt, pepper if necessary, and

then remove from the barbecue.

13. Let it rest for 5 minutes, then put on plates and serve.

Braised pork cheek with mushrooms

PREPARATION TIME: 20 minutes
COOKING TIME: 70 minutes
DIFFICULT LEVEL: Medium
CALORIES FOR 100 GRAMS: 236
FAT FOR 100 GRAMS: 10
CARBOIDRATES FOR 100 GRAMS: 4
PROTEINS FOR 100 GRAMS: 21

INGREDIENTS FOR 4 SERVINGS

- 700 grams of pork cheek
- 300 grams of mushrooms
- 1 onion
- 6 small carrots
- 200 ml of red wine
- 250 grams of tomato pulp
- 2 sprigs of rosemary
- 2 bay leaves
- 2 sage leaves
- 2 cloves
- Olive oil to taste
- Salt and pepper to taste

DIRECTIONS

1. Preheat the Pit Boss at 374 ° F for 15 minutes.
2. Preheat a cast iron saucepan for 10 minutes.
3. Peel and wash carrots and onion and then chop them.
4. Wash and dry sage, bay leaf and rosemary.
5. Wash and dry the mushrooms and then cut them into slices.
6. When the saucepan has heated up, put two tablespoons of oil to heat.
7. As soon as it is hot, put the carrots and onion to brown.
8. Add bay leaves, sage and rosemary, stir and cook for 2 minutes.
9. Now put the pork cheek and sauté for 5 minutes.

10. Put the wine and let it evaporate.
11. Add the tomato pulp and mix again.
12. Add a glass of water, season with salt and pepper and then add the cloves.
13. Now put the lid on the saucepan and cook for 60 minutes.
14. Now add the mushrooms and continue cooking for 15 minutes.
15. Now remove the casserole from the Pit Boss and let the meat rest for 5 minutes.
16. Put the meat and the cooking juices on the plates and serve.

Pork ribs on a cream of aromatic herbs

PREPARATION TIME: 20 minutes
COOKING TIME: 10 minutes
DIFFICULT LEVEL: Simple
CALORIES FOR 100 GRAMS: 322
FAT FOR 100 GRAMS: 23
CARBOIDRATES FOR 100 GRAMS: 2
PROTEINS FOR 100 GRAMS: 19

INGREDIENTS FOR 4 SERVINGS
- 8 pork chops of 150 grams each
- 1 tablespoon of smoked paprika
- 1 tablespoon of dried oregano
- Salt and pepper to taste
- Olive oil to taste

For the sauce
- 1 sprig of chopped parsley
- 1 sprig of chopped rosemary
- 2 chopped sage leaves
- 1 sprig of chopped thyme
- 100 ml of cooking cream
- 100 grams of Greek yogurt

DIRECTIONS
1. Wash and dry the pork ribs and then brush them with olive oil.
2. Sprinkle the meat with salt, pepper, paprika and oregano.
3. Preheat the Pit Boss at 374 ° F for 15 minutes with the lid closed.
4. Cook the ribs over direct heat for 5 minutes with the lid closed.
5. Turn the chops and continue cooking for another 5 minutes.
6. Just cooked, remove from the barbecue and let the ribs rest for 5 minutes.
7. In the meantime, prepare the sauce.
8. Put the cooking cream, yogurt and aromatic herbs in the glass of the blender.

9. Blend until you get a smooth and homogeneous sauce.
10. Put the chops on plates, sprinkle with the sauce and serve.

Grilled pork and sausage skewers

PREPARATION TIME: 20 minutes
COOKING TIME: 20 minutes

DIFFICULT LEVEL: Simple
CALORIES FOR 100 GRAMS: 226
FAT FOR 100 GRAMS: 18
CARBOIDRATES FOR 100 GRAMS: 1
PROTEINS FOR 100 GRAMS: 14

INGREDIENTS FOR 4 SERVINGS
- 450 grams of pork loin
- 200 grams of sausage
- 1 yellow pepper
- 8 slices of smoked bacon
- Salt and pepper to taste
- Olive oil to taste

DIRECTIONS
1. Wash the pepper, remove the seeds and white filaments and then cut them into 12 cubes.
2. Wash and dry the pork and cut it into cubes.
3. Cut the sausage into 8 pieces.
4. Wrap the pork in the bacon and start forming the skewers.
5. Take 4 metal skewers and put first a piece of sausage, then the pepper, and then the pork. Repeat the operation again and do the same with the other skewers.
6. Brush the skewers with oil and sprinkle them with salt and pepper.
7. Preheat the Pit Boss at 392 ° F for 10 minutes.
8. Place the skewers directly on the grill and cook for 4

minutes per side, turning them on all sides.

9. As soon as they are ready, remove them from the grill, immediately put them on the plates and serve.

CPSIA information can be obtained
at www.ICGtesting.com
Printed in the USA
BVHW091412070621
608934BV00002B/522